An Anthology of Tomorrow's Past

The Collected Works of Esaw Wilson, Jr.

Esaw Wilson, Jr.

Impact Learning Publications

An Anthology of Tomorrow's Past
The Collected Works of Esaw Wilson, Jr.
Copyright © 2015 by Esaw Wilson, Jr.

All rights reserved. No part of this publication may be reproduced, distributed, or transmitted in any form or by any means, including photocopying, recording, or other electronic or mechanical methods, without the prior written permission of the publisher, except in the case of brief quotations embodied in critical reviews and certain other noncommercial uses permitted by copyright law. For permission requests, write to the publisher, addressed "Attention: Permissions Coordinator," at the address below.

Published in the United States by Impact Learning Publications
PO Box 736
Tougaloo, MS 39174

First Edition, December 2015

ISBN 978-0997089707
Library of Congress Control Number: 2015959431
Cover and book design by LEAD of MS
Edited by Tameka Williams, M.Ed.

ACKNOWLEDGEMENTS

Thank you God, for you saved me. Thank you family, for you love me. Thank you friends, for you support me. Thank you readers, for you give me a voice. Thank you all.

FOREWORD

The book, *An Anthology of Tomorrow's Past,* written by Esaw Wilson, Jr., guides us through the thought process puzzles that many of us have pieced together in this experience we call life.

Wilson's poems keep us rooted in reality as his works touch on spirituality, love, and life. His word choice is clear and insightful, yet intense, purposeful, and convicting.

I strongly recommend this book as it contains relatable literary works that convey a message for every reader.

Tameka Williams, M.Ed.

To my loving wife of sixty-two years and counting…

Table of Contents

A CUP FOR YOU	2
ANGEL KNOCK	4
ASK OF YOU	5
BEAUTY QUEEN	6
BIRTHDAY	7
BLACK MARE	8
THE CALL	9
CHURCH	10
COLD WINDS	12
CONTENTED HAWK	14
DEAR MOM	16
DISMAL	18
ENVISION	19
EXPLORE	20
FAMILY	21
FANTASY	22
FOSTER DULLES	24
THE FIRST ASTRONAUT	26
FOLLOW YOU	28
FLAME	29
GENTLE BREEZE	30
GOLDEN MARE	32
GRANDMOTHER'S SAY	36
HER BEAUTY	38

HIS TOWER	39
HOUR	40
IN LOVE	42
LITTLE BIRD	44
LIVE	46
LONELY	47
LOVE SHARED	48
MAIDEN	49
MOON LIT NIGHT	50
MY CHURCH	52
MY DEAR	55
MY DEATH	56
MY FIRST BORN	58
NEWBORN	59
PARTNER	60
PRAYER	61
REALM	62
REMORSE	64
REPAY	66
SAY GRACE, FATHER	68
SECOND BORN	70
SHY LOVE	71
SLEEP ON	72
SILENT	74
SIN	76
SINNER MAN	78

SOLITUDE	81
THANKS	82
THIS LOVE	84
TRUE LOVE	85
UGLY	86
VALENTINE	87
VOYAGE	88
WED	90
THE WEDDING	91
WHY	92
YOUR HANDS	93
YOUR LOVE	94

A CUP FOR YOU

A cup for you a cup for me

A cup of coffee or a cup of tea

A quiet moment for just us two

A cup for me and a cup for you

May God continue his smiles from above

That showers us with His tender love

A casual sip a tender glance

A soft touch a sweet romance

A cup for you a cup for me

A cup of coffee or a cup of tea

May God continue to bless us two

A lifelong dream may God see us through

A tender moment of quiet bliss

A soft whisper a tender kiss

A shared dream between us two

A lifetime commitment for me and you

A cup for you a cup for me

A cup of coffee a cup of tea

A quiet moment for just us two

A merging prayer God carry us through

ANGEL KNOCK

An angel knocked on my mother's door

And much to my dismay

He carried my father into the skies

While startled eyes did gaze

As he left my mother's side

With a voice that showed no fear

He said to her in a low tone

I am leaving you my dear

Yes an angel knocked on my father's door

For his work on Earth was done

And he has gone to receive his reward

As other saints have done

ASK OF YOU

This day my dear I ask of you

To do the things I want you to do

And say the things I want to hear

To fill my suffering heart with cheer

Hold me tightly in your arms

Fill me with your many sweet charms

Kiss my lips so tenderly

To make my heart both light and free

That I might drift forever through

The star filled heavens with only you

For none these glorious moments share

Oh darling love me with tender care

With a love my darling that none can share

BEAUTY QUEEN

She waked with grace as she passed by

And one could not help but cast an eye

Upon her lovely face

And I in my place did turn to look

Upon her beauty and grace

She did not cast an eye my way

Nor did she a moment stay

Her feet were light as though in flight

As they gracefully carried her out of sight

The flowers danced to and fro

The birds sang sweet and low

The day was fair sweet was the air

Oh her beauty was showing everywhere

BIRTHDAY

Dear mom

I remember birthdays came oh so slow

And Christmas was always so far away

The old year would never go

The sun shining was always hot

Upon that dusty ground

The trees stayed green forever

Never changing to a golden brown

Now the leaves are falling from the trees

The sky is dark and gray

Christmas is almost here

Seems it just passed yesterday

Now something tells me once again

That your birthday is near

By a wintery breeze and a stormy night

I have missed it again I fear

Oh dear oh dear

BLACK MARE

Who is it that is upon that hill

Astride that dark black mare

His eyes as bright as balls of fire

His finger pointing there

I watched his victim struggle hard

Though his struggle was in vain

He forced his fleeting soul return

Only to lose it again

The rider turned around his mare

And as he rode I heard him say

No one knows when I am coming

So prepare yourself today

THE CALL

Come oh come to the church of the Lord

And He will give you rest

Come oh come to the house of God

For He will surely bless

Bring all your troubles and sorrow

These He shall receive

Bring all of your pains and woes

These He shall relieve

Pray to God for mercies

Sing glorious unto His name

He shall remove our pains

For God knows our sorrows

Our hardships and our sins

He gives us strength in weakness

He for us our battles win

CHURCH

You ask me to come dwell with you

When you put fourth so little effort to

Make me want to be a part of this

You call the house of God

You ask me to give my hand

Confess to God and take a stand

For right and truth alone with you

Yet you do the things that I do

How can I help you understand

When with so little effort you work your plan

Oh how my soul's fire kindles

Oh how small your faith it seems to dwindle

Now you say you have done your part

You come to church and worship God

But this service which strengthens you

Makes my soul sad and blue

COLD WINDS

Cold is the wind from the arctic pole

Winter rains are wet and cold

Falling snow chills the soul

And blizzards are bold

Blizzards are bold and wintery cold

Arctic winds are from the pole

That blast against my wanton soul

Chilling and filling my soul

Chill my soul to one last spark love

Remain a flame in my heart

The wind that blows from the arctic pole

The falling snow that chills my soul

The wintery rain so wet and cold

The snow filled blizzards that are so bold

The blizzards are bold and wintery cold

And arctic breezes from the pole

Beat against my wanton soul

Yet my love for you shall never grow cold

CONTENTED HAWK

He sails with ease across the sky

And beneath the clouds

Above where I sit

Watching his most graceful movement

I wonder if his soul is content

I wonder if he ever tried

To figure out who made the sky

Who sent him such a gentle breeze

To glide up above the trees

Who cast the sun up in the sky

That he might see whenever he flies

Who gave him life and liberty

A heart and soul and set him free

I pondered long in pensive mood

Without a moment's solitude

Until that bird that caught my eye

It seemed to say I try I try

It's now I know his soul is content

He knows it is God from whom its sent

DEAR MOM

Dear mom

I guess by now you are upset with me

But dates I don't remember you see

By now you must be 23

And I your son am 38

Or is it that I am forty eight

Oh dear just wait

Were you born early in June

Early morning or afternoon

Was it July August or September

Oh my dear I can't remember

Yet this voice that I do hear

Saying your birthday is near

So if I am late I want you to know

That all of us do love you so

And if the date does slip my mind

As the leaves fall from the trees in time

And the sky changes from blue to gray

And night escapes into the day

Always remember that our love for you

Is as deep as the ocean and forever true

And if ever a thought should enter your mind

Look up at the heaven and count the stars that shine

Or go to Lake Michigan with a well rounded plan

To count every tiny minute grain of sand

Yet the sand on the beach and the stars up above

Can never no not ever equal our love

DISMAL

Why are you sad my darling

If the sun has fallen from the sky

What has become of your warm smile

That scintillating gleam in your eye

Once the mornings were bright and gay

The sun rose every day

To kiss the roses on their cheeks

And to give joy to the poor and meek

As if the face of God was there

With smiles of grace and tender care

Why are you sad my darling

Am I not joy for thee

Can I not make you happy

And make your heart light and free

If these things I cannot do

Then God forgive me for hurting you

ENVISION

As you go through these trying times

Let us pray to God above

To give you strength and courage

To enfold you in His love

And when you are a mother

Which won't be very long

May your children always greet you

Every morning with a song

And always remember

Dearest daughter never fear

For your mom and I adore you

And our love is always near

EXPLORE

Should I explore the fairest light

That's seen in the heavens on the darkest night

And pause a moment for silent prayer

I'm sure I'll find God waiting there

Should I explore beneath the sea

So deep that light no eyes can see

And ask my God to please take care

I know his eyes will see me there

FAMILY

When this face of mine was sad

Loneliness it did show

But today it's bubbling over

Filled with happiness once more

No more sorry lonely moments

No more red eyes filled with tears

Only happiness around me

For the love one's I adore

Ida Valerie Edgar and Kenneth

Be with me forever more

FANTASY

Night fall and dreams of you

Of beauty of love

That must come true

Less this sad heart of mine do break

Beneath love's weight

For lover's sake

Ah does love have this power

It seems to me my dreams are gone

But love for you still lingers on

With each moment my heart does ache

Come back my love for lover's sake

For my heart shall break this hour

FOSTER DULLES

The bells are toiling sad and long

The sky is dark and gray

The flags are flying at half mast

The Horner guard taps they play

The soldiers marching slowly by

Their officers are saluting

And on the command to fire

The rifle men are shooting

Other storm clouds did gather

Long before this day of yore

And this great man did weather

All that human clouds could pour

Foster Dulles has left us

Gone to answer a higher call

May we never stop remembering

How he fought to save us all

Still the rifle men are shooting

Still the flags fly at half mast

For this great man who has for us fought

So nobly at his task

THE FIRST ASTRONAUT

I sat upon the fires of hell

My heart chuckled with delight

I sat upon the fires of hell

And prayed with all my soul and might

I sat upon the fires of hell

And heard her billows row

I felt her kick beneath my seat

I heard her angry bellow

Yes I sat upon the fires of hell

And rode her above the trees

And high above the mountain tops

Over clouds and beyond the breeze

I rode upon the fires of hell

High into the heavens above

I rode her till her fires were out

She was as gentle as a dove

Then knowing she could not break my will

Nor twist me to her delight

She deposited me beneath the golden moon

On a heavenly star filled night

Yes I rode upon the fires of hell

And much to my delight

She deposited me beneath the golden moon

On a heavenly star filled night

FOLLOW YOU

If man should stare and wonder

How such could ever be

That such a maiden with star like eyes

Did fall in love with me

Take heed but do not fret

For your love shall come some day

And with an understanding heart

She will follow you away

For no one knows nor understands

What God has for you or me

The working of His mighty hand

His love so deep we cannot see

FLAME

Don't make me cry dear

For life itself is a pain

And the added burden of love and joy combines

To put my heart in a flame

Don't make me shy dear

For I do love you so

And to hear you say that we must part

Caused the flames in my heart to glow

GENTLE BREEZE

If love was but the sunshine

And joy was but the breeze

And all the things of love and joy

Was but the birds and bees

Then happy am I

For I am sure you see

That you are the golden sunshine

And the gentle breeze is me

And all the singing of the birds

And buzzing of the bees

Are they that God has sent us

To show that he is pleased

GOLDEN MARE

I leaped upon a golden mare

She dashed across the sky

High hope had I of a faraway place

Where hopes and dreams did aspire

I rode above the snow white clouds

Over valleys trees and dales

And out into the far beyond

Its future none can tell

We passed above the golden moon

And above the red hot sun

And off into the dark blue sky

Where brilliant stars do run

I drew my breath as we approached

a crave a starry bay

She leaped across to the other side

And hurried on her way

My hopes and dreams I passed them all

As I rode that golden mare

I watched them pass beneath her feet

As she hurried through the air

My friends my neighbors my relatives

I passed along the way

And as I rode into the night

I heard my grandmother say

Come back come back my son

Do not go away

Stay with your wife and children son

They need you more each day

The dark blue night drew darker

The stars did pass away

The golden mare grew faded

Her feet began to stay

She paused beside a dusty road

In a town named Despair

She bowed her head she galloped away

And left me standing there

And galloped up the dusty road

To God I know not where

And as I stand beside this dusty road

I find I'm in despair

I find myself longing for the thing

I left back there

And now I pray each night long before the down

The golden mare will come my way

And home again we'll run

Oh golden mare please come my way

Don't leave me in despair

Dear God hear my cry

Send back that golden mare

GRANDMOTHER'S SAY

I heard my grandmother say

Son don't forget to pray

Thank God for the blessings He sends you every day

Son don't forget to pray

I heard my grandmother say

Son life for me won't be long

Death will come for this old tired body

And God will take me home

Son life for me won't be long

I heard my grandmother say

I am going to my heavenly home

Son I have loved my enemy and my neighbor

Son I have done nobody wrong

I am going home

I heard my grandmother say

Just waiting on the Lord

Son I have suffered trials and tribulations

While on this Earth I have trod

Son I am waiting on the Lord

I am waiting on the Lord son

Life for me won't be long son

Thank God every day son

Don't forget to pray son

Don't forget to pray

HER BEAUTY

Her beauty is like the lustrous star

Viewed from high above the mountain top

Where man made objects are unseen

Human noises are void and the air is clean

And filled with fragrance of wild cherry blossoms of the early spring

Her eyes twinkle like the distant stars

High up in the heavens

As seen on the darkest night

When no moon shows its form over the distant horizon

Her lips are like the summer breeze

That sweeps the valley to crest the lilies

And causes the daffodils to dance

While filling the valley with softly plaid melodies

I saw her once and then no more

For such beauty is not for mortal eyes to see

For such was made for immortals to cress to kiss

To love for evermore

HIS TOWER

The Lord is in his holy tower

Yet He is with us this hour

In this cup that we now take

In this bread that we now break

In the air that we now breath

Strength He gives for our spiritual needs

Yes the Lord be in his holy tower

Watching over his lovely flowers

Guarding them from the wintery breeze

Protecting them with the fallen leaves

The Lord is in his holy tower

Are you close to him this hour

Do you fit into his plan

Of baptism under his holy command

HOUR

I sat upon a hill today and observed an hour went by

I singled out of all things the creatures that could fly

I watched the birds flying high sailing on the breeze

And sometimes they fell out of the sky to land in the trees

I saw a lovely butterfly bobbing across the way

He stopped at every lovely flower that in his path did lay

A honey bee came buzzing by he is in a rush I'd say

He has a lot of work to do before the passing of day

Mr wasp built his nest just above my head

He has a lot of work to do before he goes to bed

Smaller things I did hear than Mr honey bee

They only sang in my ear but them I did not see

A big mosquito stopped by and gave me one big bite

But he I must confess did lose his daily fight

I was content upon that hill in the shade of a big oak tree

I knew that I was not alone God was there with me

And I thought of all the time the hours and the pain

It must have taken God to make every little thing

Content was I for just one hour now the noisy sky

The thunder roaring of human power noisy man flew by

IN LOVE

To hold you in my arms
To press you close to me
To whisper sweet love phrases
To kiss you tenderly

The sparkle in your eye
The softness of your cheek
Your warmth your beauty
No other love I seek

To hear you whisper softly
In a sweet earnest tone
I love you oh I love you
I'll never do you wrong

Oh darling how I miss
The softness of your kiss
Oh darling how I long
To be forever in love like this

LITTLE BIRD

If I was a little bird locked in a cage

I would never sing out of my heart to show that I am brave

I would only sit and cry all day my owners would surely say

I've never seen a little bird not ever cheerful or gay

They would wonder why I would never lift up my head and sing

Or why I would never fly upon my little swing and swing

They would never seem to understand that to live is to be free

To do the things you want to do like flying from the top of a tree

Or flying across the open air to glide upon the breeze

Or greet the morning sun from a home of sticks grass and leaves

Yes I would pine away my life there behind those little bars

And never see the rising sun nor glance at the midnight stars

I would never see a thunder cloud or feel the chill of snow

Or see the beautiful flowers in bloom or the evening sunset glow

But when my life is finally spent and I am put to rest at last

My only prayer is that I'm laid in an open field of grass

Where the sun can warm my breast and the rain can soak my skin

Where I am returned unto the Earth to be born once again

Then all the things I have wanted to see I am sure I will see at last

For God will care for me in my open field of grass

LIVE

As the night that is about me no twinkle no stars

No moon no light but dark

So are his eyes dark

As the door that stands before me is bared

Locked and bolted

So are his lips bared

As the clock that does not chime and will not chime

And cannot chime nor tick is stopped

So has his heart stopped

Though his eyes are dark as the night is dark

Though his lips are bared as the door is bared

Though his heart has stopped as the clock is stopped

Yet he lives he liveth eternally with God.

LONELY

Do you say that I am lonely

Do you say that I am sad

Nay my friend I will tell you only

Though I cry my heart is glad

The tears are for the lonely hours

I have been away from home

Laboring for the lovely flowers

And the rose I call my own

Working so that the day come nearer

We will all together be

LOVE SHARED

I send these lines

With all my love

With heart and hope

I pray to Him above

That no matter how far apart we be

Through space and distance

Our love can see

And with each moment of silent prayer

My love finds you

What love we share

MAIDEN

Have you seen a lovely maiden

    Her age is twenty two

With eyes as bright as the noon day sun

    Cheeks as soft as the morning dew

No she is only twenty one

    A year too many was I

She wore white clouds upon her feet

    Her garment was like a starry blue sky

I know her age now my friend

    She is only twenty

For I have seen her again and now

    She is my own you see

MOON LIT NIGHT

Once beneath the moon lit sky

I watched the stars light up your eyes

I watched the moonlight in your hair

And kissed your lips while setting there

The night was calm the night was fair

The moon did glitter on your hair

The star's twinkle in your eyes

Then cupid let his arrow fly

The stars the moon and cupid

Who shot his arrow straight and true

The arrow passed through my chest

And lodged itself in your lovely breast

Stars fell from the sky

And found their way into those beautiful eyes

The summer breeze began to blow

Your moon lit hair danced with a glow

My heart did pound my blood did rise

I held you close you closed your eyes

Cupid chuckled and off he went

The wink of his eye gave his consent

MY CHURCH

I passed a church of those who care

And cars were parked everywhere

People standing all around

Waiting for the chord to sound

That call them to their morning prayer

This was a church of those who care

A voice within my soul did say

God have my church be this way

Have cars parked all around

And members waiting to hear the sound

That call us to our morning prayer

So others may know how much we care

And some day through humbleness or pride

Come in and with us abide

But as I drew near my door

That light within me that did glow

Began to flutter and fade away

There are fewer here the voice did say

Fewer here to worship God

To walk the path that Jesus trod

Who carried the cross to Calvary

Who died that all might be free

Fewer fewer my soul did say

Oh God so few this Easter day

Oh how I suffered while sitting there

Oh God where are the ones who care

Where are the ones who promised thee

To serve thee faithfully until eternity

The ones down these isles did trod

To give the pastor their hand and you their heart

Dear God this last thing I pray

Help us to do our part each day

Help us to on Sunday morn

Arise with the morning sun

And come to church someone might say

I passed church where those who love and care

Faithfully carry on God's services there

MY DEAR

Love me dear

If not please stay away because

Every time I see you my heart flies away

Want me dear

If not leave me alone

Return my heart unto it's place get out and be gone

For only when I see you or know that you are near

Does valiant love over take me

Gurr! I'll get you yet my dear

MY DEATH

When I am gone my dearest

When death shall come for me

Plant me not in a box of steel nor concrete

Nor lead but let it be

A tree that hued in early June

And dried in the summer

Air and drake with linden dark and sheen

And covered with dark purple hair

For I am just a simple man

With few of the world's goods

And when I am gone I want to be laid

In a simple box of wood

For when eternal life shall come

To take me from my tomb

I shall not awake to find that I am trapped

In steel that spells my doom

For who can say that eternal life

Is not a simple thing

As the rolling grass where the cattle graze

Or the bread that's made from grain

Or the nuts and fruits that the trees give

Or the greens and beans from the farmer's field

Or the fish that swim in the ocean deep

Or the eagle perched upon the mountain peak

Just a simple wooden box is all I desire

So when eternal life comes I can fly fly fly

MY FIRST BORN

I gazed upon her

Beautiful was she there

For she was my delight

A thousand moonbeams in her hair

Her eyes were star bright

Her face as soft as rose buds

Under a blanket of morning dew

Her lips as red as cherry

Unkissed I know that's true

How beautiful you are my little one

So young so free so fair

You will always be the fellow's ideal

So never let your morals down

We will always pray

That God will help you keep your feet on solid ground

NEWBORN

Eyes of twinkling stars

Cheeks of blushing pink

Skin soft as a gentle breeze

Tears sweet enough to drink

How wonderful to watch you lying there

How loving God must be

To send you down from Heaven

To be with Bell and me

Grow strong my little one

For strong you must be

To run to jump to lift and play

And live life fancy free

How wonderful to watch her

Growing up towards the sky

To know that God has sent her

To be with Bell and I

PARTNER

Where would I be today

> Perhaps still trying to find my way
>
> Among the thorns and pitfalls of life
>
> Losing my footing more than twice

Where would you be today

> Had you not known this man
>
> Perhaps in some dark backwards place
>
> Or drifting with the shifting sands

Sleep on my partner Earnie

> Rest in your eternal place
>
> Your name shall never be forgotten
>
> Though we may forget your face

PRAYER

I come to thee oh God

For I know that I have sinned

I know that I have done you wrong

And have wronged my fellow man

Forgive me oh God

For the sins that I have done today

Teach me how to live for you Lord

And touch me when I go astray

Bless all of mankind oh God

Show us how to do your will

Help us spread the good news

So that empty souls can be filled

REALM

I know the place I would like to be

Where the breezes blow and the air is free

From dust smoke and stuffiness

That industrial towns and cities processed

There life is quiet sweet and calm

The birds sing and rabbits run

There trees grow tall toward the sky

All that is seen does please the eye

Often when I am blessed with solitude

Alone where none can intrude

My thoughts drift to that Heaven of rest

For peace for quiet for contentness

Although ages pass as does the breeze

And man destroys to satisfy his needs

The place of quiet content

Thank God I am blessed I am blessed

REMORSE

I killed my father though not with sword nor gun

But with my every walk in life

Through deeds I have or have not done

My father is dead I am to blame

He died of a broken heart

I am ashamed

Oh how many times can I say

I sent him a card on his birthday

Or took the time to write a line

To ask if he is feeling fine

Or saw a tie upon the shelf

That I decided for him and not myself

Yes I killed my father

Through selfishness and greed

So if your father lives today

Take heed my friend take heed

REPAY

Sometimes I wonder if this could be
The life that God has meant for me
A life of love and happiness
A lovely angel in my breast
And when my thoughts of life are spent
I'd find that I am content
To know your love is ever near
To fill my lonely heart with cheer
What have I to give in return
For such a love I have not earned
But have obtained by God's consent
To be my life time compliment
I have searched and searched
But cannot find
A solemn deed to ease my mind
No single gift have I spent
To secure this blessed compliment
Oh God I cry aloud to thee
Open my eyes that I may see
The means by which I am to pay
For blessings that you continually send my way

Oh God oh God am I to be

A constant bore a burden to thee

Am I always to receive

And never repay in one kind deed

I wonder if its only me

Are there others who cannot see

Who have searched and searched but cannot find

Or understand why God is so kind

Or cannot recall some deed he has done

For God himself or for someone

No single answer can I find

To say for this God has been kind

And yet each day his gifts flow free

Of life of health of liberty

Of rain and sun of summer breeze

Of sweet smelling blossoms and fruitful trees

SAY GRACE, FATHER

How many times I'd cry last night

Just to see his loving face

Oh how I strained into the night

To see him at his place

And strained my ears with bowed head

To hear him say *the grace*

How wonderful my heart would feel

To awake come the day

To stand in church with bowed head

And listen to him pray

Or sit in class with other lads

As we have often done

While he explained from Genesis

How God made the sun

Or chased me across the grassy fields

Around my grandmother's house

Or together we would set a trap

To catch a naughty mouse

Or return again to that Christmas night

As we played on the floor

And listened to their voices

Mom and Santa at the door

Oh Christmas shall be sad for me

For I shall not see his face

Nor hear him bless the sacrament

Nor hear him say *the grace*

SECOND BORN

Often I wonder of the robin

        Singing in the nearest tree

Often I wonder of the firefly

        Flashing so that it can see

Now I wonder more concerning

        As I watch you laying there

I find myself saying oh how God does answer prayer

        To us he has been generous

With a girl who is long pass three

        And now a boy who is just a babe

Who his dad would love to see

SHY LOVE

What kind of love have I

To take it

And pit her from my eye

And say to others

There is my love

But always pass her by

What kind of love is this

That I have sealed with a kiss

Yet none can say there is his love

Or show our love exist

SLEEP ON

How do you rest in that grave
How can your soul be gay
With all the tons of dirt that laid
Upon your chest that way

How can you when the morning come
See the sunrise from the east
Or hear the birds with their lovely songs
Or the noises made by beast

I ask you sir down in that hole
Is this your life span end
Have you lost your eternal soul
Never to regain it again

Have you loved your fellow man
Or helped a friend in need

Saved some soul from lusty ways
From the treacherous ways of sin

Or kneel and pray and shout God's praise
Rise up to be born again
Say yes my friend and I will know
For I do understand

Though death may come and go
You shall return again
For God shall come to Earth again
With the sealed book in his hand
Over the kingdoms shall He reign
With justice for every man

SILENT

Silent silent let thy heart be still
Silent silent for God's unchanging will

    Speaks to you in His soft tone
    To your heart His will shall be known

Silent silent get thy heart right
Pray silent softly so that God might

    Find your heart with an open door
    There His goodness and mercies might be stored

Silent now so that God may speak
To the wanton soul that does seek

    His truth His love His tender care
    That abides with us everywhere

Be silent now friends and pray
That God be with us all the way

> For He all of our sorrows share
> He all of our burdens bare
> He our heart aches receive
> He our sufferings relieve

SIN

Could this be the greatest sin

To have and not to share

God's love and joy with other men

Whose souls have not grown to care

Could I be guilty and yet not know

Of trying to hide my life light glow

To know and love God strongly within

And still hide it from other men

No this can never be

For God will forever show His loving light for men to see

Though the barrier may know

SINNER MAN

If I was a leader God
This is what I would do
I would tell all of my followers
To follow you
I would in my every dealings
Strive for your command
I would not make a move God
Until you took my hand
If I was a leader
God you understand
I'm not a leader I'm just a sinful man

If I was a Christian God
This is what I would do
I'd stand along the byways
And convert mankind to you

I would live in every way
So that everyone can see
Thou living son Jesus
Living again in me
If I was a Christian
God you understand
I'm not a Christian I'm just a sinner man

If I was a preacher God
This is what I'd do
I'd build a great cathedral
And name it after you
And everyone who passed its door
Would surely understand
That this is God's cathedral
Built by a Christian man
If I was a preacher
God you understand
I'm not a preacher I'm just a sinner man

I'm just a sinner man God
And all that I will do
Is go to church on Sunday
And give a buck or two

I go to church on Sunday God
And dwell with fellow man
And listen to the sermon
And shake the preacher's hand

But you understand
I don't go every Sunday God
Cause I'm just a sinner man

SOLITUDE

A night that's filled with brilliant stars

As far as the eye can see

And in its midst one little cloud

That's out of harmony

The night is calm warm and fair

The air is sweet and free

But that one motionless cloud

Did cast its spell on me

I know not from where it came

Or how it came to be

Or why it hung its lifeless form

There for my eyes to see

Somehow I am like this cloud

I am out of harmony

Among these bright and flashing lights

Where mortal men run free

THANKS

Dear Lord and Father of us all

We thank thee for thou grace

We thank thee for thou righteousness

We thank thee for thou place

We thank thee for thou tender heart

Which gives us hope today

We thank thee for thou sweet love

That you show in every way

We thank thee for that blessed day

When thou son was sent to Earth

We thank thee for the prophets the star

The angels singing of his birth

We thank thee for his gentleness

That touched the lives of man

We thank him for his love for us

That made us a part of your plan

We thank thee for the life he lived

His death on Calvary

For he lived to show us the way

And died to set us free

THIS LOVE

This love I have for you

Is as broad as the wide wide sea

A love that is deep and true

As lasting as a redwood tree

A love that outshines by far

The brightest and largest star

Although night shall come

And hide your face

And I awake in some ungodly place

Yet fear of death shall not erase

Nor cause my love for you to waste

TRUE LOVE

Tell me that you are mine
And that your love is true
Tell me that your lips meet only mine
And never on others

Tell me that as time passes along
As seasons come and go
That no other arms you will find
No other love you will know
I am sure that your love is true

For our love grows stronger through the years
And though suffering and pain may come
Our love will outlast all of our tears

UGLY

Kiss me oh my loving dear
Draw me close to thee
Tell me how much you missed the sight
Of homely me

Look my darling into my eyes
Say in a soft sweet tone
It's true my ugly duckling
I'm glad to have you home

Hold me close my lovely one
So close you cannot see
This ugly harrowed righting face
That only hid from thee

For the world called me a wonder
The kids all run and hide
But to you my loving rose bud
I am your joy and pride

VALENTINE

I would not buy a greeting card
To say these things to you
What I feel within my heart
For a card would not do

                              I would not buy a book of poems
                                      To tell you how I feel
                        For the things that a card maker would say
                                For me would not be real

For what is real is life and love
And beauty and sweet and truth
And warmth and kindness and thoughtfulness
These all add up to you

                                      So I ask you at this time
                                      In my simple little way
                                      Will you be my valentine
                                      On this valentine's day

VOYAGE

It is the night upon the ocean
And the clouds of ghostly doom
Race across the yellow flickering
Of the bright and golden moon

Cast their shadows upon the ocean yeah
Their ghostly shadows passed
The ship the haunted vessel
Like a strain of angel hair

Ghostly gleam that golden moonlight
Cast upon the ghostly sea
Gaily flickers across the ocean
Joyfully jingling unto me

And the ghostly clouds of heaven
Cast their shadows across the sea
As if someone is running jumping
Throwing their ghostly thrills at me

And the ship she split the water
And the course they think is right
Still the ghostly domain shadow
Filled me with the ghostly night

WED

With this ring **I** do wed thee
Forever and a day
Forever is for all my life
The day when I am passed away
To rest in holy sleep
My love for you shall never die
And I shall forever be true
For with this ring I tie
To bin**d** and be bound by you
Until eternity shall come
Only God shall part us two

THE WEDDING

The ship is launched her sails are set
The sky bright and blue
The ocean calm the wind fair
Her course straight and true
They left the land that was home
To venture out to sea
They left the warmth of mother's love
To set out to be free
Love sweet love set sail this day
With hope and joy divine
Youth sweet youth set sail this day
To wait the passing of time
And we are left standing on the shore
With hopeful hearts do pray
That love sweet love will grow stronger
As the hair on their heads turn gray
That love sweet love will bind them
On their island in the sun
When the sky turns black and the winds howl
And the dreaded hurricane run

WHY

Why are you here sir
I am here because of curiosity
To try and find out just what God means to me
I have searched wherever I have gone
I have talked to men who should have known
The life God intends us to live
His utmost plan
And yet still do not understand
Just why God made man
Maybe while here with you
I will find a faith that's good and true
I will find out what God really means
And see the things as of yet unseen
Why are you here I ask you sir
What are you watching waiting for
Could it be that you don't understand
Just why God made man

YOUR HANDS

I have no hands to do my will
No hands to reach out and touch the ill
No hands to soothe away their pains
No hands to the world the gospel bring
No hands to hold the wanton babe
No hands to lower gently into the grave
No hands but yours my work to do
Your hands must carry the world my truth

YOUR LOVE

Darling what would you do
If I would give the world to you
Would you take the stars above
And in return give me true love
If I could take a world of gold
And place it in a heavenly mold
And make for you a golden dove
Would you then give me your love

ABOUT THE AUTHOR

Esaw Wilson Jr was born and raised in Jackson MS in 1928. A poet, a retired business owner, and a retired soldier in the military, Wilson met and married his wife, Ida Bell, over sixty-two years ago. During his attendance at Lanier High School, Wilson was drafted into the Army and traveled aboard the USS Searburb heading to Korea. It was in those days that he was inspired to write his first poem, *Voyage*. Since then, all of his poems have been inspired by events and people in which his path has crossed.

www.ingramcontent.com/pod-product-compliance
Lightning Source LLC
LaVergne TN
LVHW051526070426
835507LV00023B/3336